Bhagavad Gita

(Rendered into simple English)

O.P. GHAI

with a Foreword by
M.P. Pandit

New Dawn

NEW DAWN
An imprint of Sterling Publishers (P) Ltd.
A-59 Okhla Industrial Area, Phase-II,
New Delhi-110020.
Tel: 26387070, 26386209 Fax: 91-11-26383788
E-mail: ghai@nde.vsnl.net.in
www.sterlingpublishers.com

Bhagavad Gita
©2003, Sterling Publishers Private Limited
ISBN 81 207 2538 7

Published by Sterling Publishers Pvt. Ltd., New Delhi-110020.
Lasertypeset by Vikas Compographics, New Delhi-110020.
Printed at Shagun Offset, New Delhi-110029.

Contents

Foreword

The Bhagavad Gita is rightly considered to be the most popular of the Hindu scriptures of India. It has been translated into all the major languages of the world. It is perhaps the most commented upon epic poem by scholars, laymen and mystics. Each commentator approaches the Gita from his own angle and extracts from it what supports his position. It is thus that the various schools of Vedanta have interpreted the Gita. And indeed, each approach has its own justification.

The present exposition by Shri O.P.Ghai proceeds from no preconceived positions. The Gita has grown in him during his study of over forty-five years and naturally formed his guiding principles in life.

Self-made man that he is, the writer has sought from the Gita what help it offers to the modern man in a crashing world where values are discarded without compunction and success is lauded as right. In what way is the Gita a guide to happy living? As he states in his Introduction, "The Bhagavad Gita presents the Science of Being and the Art of Living. It is a complete guide to mastering the problems of day-to-day life—indispensable to any man in any age. The teachings of the Gita inspire all to realise the reality within them. True fulfilment lies in the simultaneous development of the heart and the mind."

What is most appealing about this work is the easy manner in which the high thought of the Gita is told: the narrative combines the story with the instruction in a charming way. Free from pedantry, it is a summarised version rendered in simple English with taste and aesthetic grace. All the main topics are touched upon in such a way that the reader is irresistibly drawn to the original text. Shri Ghai is well known for his constructive spirit in all his undertakings, which are considerable. It is but natural that the one feature that appeals to him most in the Gita is its spirit of reconciliation. The Gita, he would say, is no battlefield for the philosophies of Jnana Marga, Bhakti Marga, Karma Marga and other paths. Lord Krishna shows the way to integrate them in oneself and arrive at a total fulfilment. He justifies action done in consecration, bhakti. He values knowledge, jnana, as it leads to selfless love for God and for God's creation. Having practised the Gita's gospel of action in his own life, Shri Ghai carries conviction. May the readers of this slender volume share in the Light and Love that he has gained by his dedication to the Lord and his utterance.

M.P. Pandit
Sri Aurobindo Ashram
Pondicherry

Preface

I bought my first copy of the Bhagavad Gita forty-five years ago. It was a publication of Gita Press, Gorakhpur, priced at 4 annas (25 paise). I was twenty-five then. I read and re-read it for a number of years but without fully understanding the message of this great epic poem.

Since then I have read several other translations and interpretations of the Gita, thirty-eight to be precise, in my efforts to grasp its lofty philosophy. Every time I read it I felt there should have been a simpler version of this celebrated epic. The idea of a simpler Gita had been at the back of my mind all those years and I had hoped someone would write a commentary easy enough for a person of average ability to appreciate it. It never occurred to me that I could also attempt a summarised rendering in simple English for laymen, young people, and foreigners not conversant with the cultural heritage of India.

It was on the first of January 1989 that I made up my mind to undertake such a task, translating the Gita's eighteen chapters in eighteen consecutive days. I started writing its first chapter on January 4 at 3.30 a.m.

I made up my mind to do a chapter a day. I awoke any time between 3 and 4 a.m. and continued writing till I had finished the chapter. It strengthened my belief in the saying that 'you can accomplish anything if you think you can'. The book was completed as scheduled.

I have only read the English version of the Gita by Indian and foreign scholars as I do not know the Sanskrit language. While writing the book I was fully aware that any translation, however competent, cannot convey the beauty and force of the original. I was also aware of my own limitations, being neither a scholar nor a philosopher. Therefore, I may be forgiven for any lapses that may have crept into the book.

I hope that more and more Indians and people from all over the world who do not have the time, the inclination or the facility to read the bigger volumes written on the Gita will be able to understand its teachings which have been presented in this book in an easily understandable form for the average reader. I also hope that it will help those who go through its pages carefully to lead a better life and make the world a better place to live in. Its practical philosophy of life will teach them how to live in this world full of stress, strain, sorrow and suffering, and yet remain calm.

The Gita's philosophy of doing one's duty has universal appeal. Its ethical aspect is a source of inspiration to one and all, irrespective of religion and country. It has become an ambassador of goodwill and understanding between the East and the West, the old world of thought and the new world of action. The Bhagavad Gita embodying the philosophy of the Vedas and the Mahabharata is the quintessence of true wisdom and a great contribution of India to the spiritual heritage of mankind.

I must say I have thoroughly enjoyed reading the Gita all my life. It has immensely helped and inspired me to do the right thing whenever I was in a difficult situation. I am convinced it will also help the reader in mastering the problems of day-to-day life.

Having based my effort on other English versions I will be failing in my duty if I do not express my gratitude to those writers whose works I have consulted and studied again and again.

O.P. Ghai

15

Acknowledgements

I am thankful to all the writers whose works I have consulted in the preparation of this book. All of them have been listed in the bibliography.

I am equally thankful to Shri R.K. Kakar, who has with love and devotion edited the manuscript with great care.

I am also thankful to Ms. Sudesh Kachroo, who prepared a flawless copy for the Press.

Last but not least, I acknowledge the deep debt of gratitude I owe to Shri M.P. Pandit, the great philosopher and

author of over seventy books who has
written an inspiring foreword to the
book. I am indeed obliged to him.

Introduction

The Bhagavad Gita (lit., 'the Lord's Song') forms part of the Mahabharata, the greatest epic poem of India, which is probably the longest in the world, containing well over one hundred thousand couplets. The Gita, composed about 2,500 years ago, comprises a dialogue between Krishna the "charioteer" and Arjuna, his *chela* (disciple) on the highest spiritual teaching.

It would take the reader only a couple of hours to go through the text of the *Gita* – and about the same time to read this book.

The subjects discussed in the discourse are knowledge, action and devotion. Krishna teaches the synthesis of all the three courses that are open to human beings. Action being the easiest of the spiritual paths, he lays more stress on it.

The quintessence of Krishna's teaching is the practice of self-control, selfless work and surrender to God. These form the foundations of happiness and peace of mind. In short, the Bhagavad Gita presents the Science of Being and the Art of Living. It is a complete guide to mastering the problems of day-to-day life — indispensable to all human beings in all ages. The teachings of the Gita inspire all to realise the reality within them. True fulfilment lies in the simultaneous development of the heart and the mind. The Gita presents the timeless wisdom and a way of life by following which any person, irrespective of his/her faith, culture or nationality, can enjoy the blessings of the paths of knowledge, action and devotion.

The Bhagavad Gita is a book of light, love and life: Jnana, Bhakti and Karma. Karma is work and work is life. The Bhagavad Gita teaches us how to be, how to think and how to act.

Arjuna's Distress

I

Alas, we have resolved to commit a great sin as we are ready to kill our friends and relatives out of greed for the pleasures of a kingdom.

Verse-45

It would be far better for me if the sons of Dhritarashtra, with weapons in hand, should kill me in the battle without any armed resistance on my part.

Verse-46

Long long ago King Pandu was the ruler of Hastinapur, a kingdom which flourished near Delhi, the present-day capital of India. He died an untimely death, leaving behind five minor sons. Before he died he entrusted the throne to his brother Dhritarashtra. He told him to give the kingdom back to his sons when they grew up.

Dhritarashtra was blind. He had one hundred sons of whom Duryodhana was the eldest. Kind-hearted, he kept the five sons of his brother in the palace in the company of his own sons. He appointed Drona to teach them the art of warfare. The Pandu brothers — Yudhishtra, Bhima, Arjuna, Nakul and

Sahadev — grew up to be great warriors. They were far superior to Dhritarashtra's sons who were called Kauravas. Dhritarashtra named Yudhishtra, the eldest of the Pandu brothers, as heir apparent to the throne.

Duryodhana, the eldest of the hundred Kaurava brothers, did not like this decision of his father favouring his cousin Yudhishtra. He became jealous and began to plot against the Pandus. His maternal uncle Shakuni helped him in his wicked designs. He advised him to invite Yudhishtra to a game of dice which he would play on Duryodhana's behalf. He would ensure Duryodhana winning it, by hook or by crook.

Yudhishtra agreed to play and, as was to be expected, he lost everything at stake: his jewels, his brothers, his kingdom and even his wife Draupadi. Duryodhana, the winner, sent the Pandus into exile for twelve years, after which they were to spend another year incognito. They lived in the forest for thirteen years braving the hardships of a rough life. Back in Hastinapur they sent a message to Dhritarashtra asking for the return of their kingdom. Dhritarashtra wanted to do so but his eldest son Duryodhana stood in the way, saying, "No, I will not give them even one inch of the kingdom." Dhritarashtra, being blind, was helpless. Even his wife Gandhari failed to persuade her son to honour the wishes of his father. This paved the way for the great battle of Mahabharata that was to be fought in the plains of Kurukshetra, about 120 km from Delhi, for eighteen days.

Yudhishtra told his brothers to get ready for the battle. Krishna, the head of the Yadava clan, offered to mediate between the cousins. When all efforts for a peaceful solution failed, a war between the Kauravas and the Pandavas became inevitable.

Yudhishtra's army comprised seven divisions, each under the charge of one of the kings who were his friends. Krishna joined the battle on the Pandava side. Arrayed against them was Duryodhana at the head of the Kaurava army of eleven divisions. He had with him great warriors like Drona, Bhishma, Karna and Ashavthama. They deployed their forces in a semi-circle. Both the armies faced each other, the commanders of the divisions riding their chariots. All preparations for the war were now complete.

The battlefield swarmed with warriors in uniform armed with bows and arrows. Thumping of elephants and horses and blowing of cymbals, trumpets and conchshells mingled with war-cries to herald the beginning of fighting. Krishna was the charioteer of Arjuna, the younger brother of Yudhishtra.

Arjuna requested Krishna to move the chariot to the centre of the battlefield so that he could view the rival forces.

Krishna drove the chariot forward and Arjuna saw his kith and kin, his uncles, granduncles, teachers, maternal uncles, cousins, sons and grandsons and friends and well-wishers facing him. He was overcome with compassion.

Arjuna was trembling. His *gandiva*, the bow given to him by one of the gods, slipped from his hands. He was shaking with grief born of conflict between the demands of the heart and the mind. He was torn between love and duty, his heart full of love for his relations and his mind ringing with the call of duty.

Seeing him in this condition, Krishna asked him what the matter was. Arjuna said, "What is the use of fighting against my own family members? I see no good in killing my kinsmen in battle. What, even if I win? Will it give me peace? Will it give me happiness? What will be the ultimate gain?" His head whirled with questions to which he could find no answers.

Arjuna said his cousins saw no wrong in fighting and destroying the family but he would not like to fall in their footsteps. They were ruled by greed and passion, unmindful of the evil they were committing. He said he knew that slaying them would be a sin. He would prefer being slain by them to slaying them. He would uphold righteousness rather than deal a blow to it.

Saying this, Arjuna sank down in his chariot seat. He dropped his bow and arrows, his mind full of grief.

The Way to the Ultimate Reality of Life

II

The man who is not disturbed by the contacts of the senses with their objects, who is even-minded in pain and pleasure and who is steadfast makes fit for eternal life.

Verse-15

You have control over your action and not over its fruits. You should not live for the fruits of action, nor attach yourself to inaction.

Verse-47

Arjuna was deep in sorrow. His mind and heart were in conflict. He could not decide whether to love or wage war against his relatives. He had tears in his eyes.

Seeing him in anguish, Shri Krishna asked him the reason for his despondency in the hour of crisis. He told Arjuna his being in low spirits was a matter of disgrace for a warrior. This unmanliness did not become him. He should give up faint-heartedness and get ready for the battle.

Arjuna told Shri Krishna there was nothing to gain from killing Bhishma and Drona. Both were his teachers and worthy of respect and reverence. This unwillingness to kill them shows Arjuna's greatness and nobility of character. He was not clear in his mind whether he should or should not fight. As he could not think of the right thing to do, he asked Shri Krishna for divine guidance. Without waiting for an answer he told Shri Krishna he would not fight.

Shri Krishna noticed the utter confusion in which Arjuna was torn between the conflicting demands of love and duty. He told Arjuna that he was a wise man and was grieving over nothing. He should not worry about the living or the dead, for his real self, the Atman, the soul, is immortal and eternal. It leaves the worn-out body just as human beings cast off worn-out clothes and take on new ones. The soul cannot be slain, it is indestructible. It is not slain when the body is slain, and therefore he should not grieve for the dead. Change is the law of life and the wise and the learned are not deluded by it. They take life as it comes.

The death of him who is born is certain and so is the rebirth of him who dies. He brought home to him the truth about the everlasting nature of the spirit and the permanent and ultimate reality of life. Arjuna's duty was not to worry about anything but to rise, face the inevitable and fight.

Shri Krishna reminded Arjuna that as a warrior his duty to fight mattered much more than the fairness of the fight and that if he shirked it he would be committing a sin. If he did not fight, both his friends and his foes would call him a coward, and that would bring him ill-fame which was worse than death. He should treat pleasure and pain, gain and loss, victory and defeat alike and get ready for the battle. This would save him from the sin he would be committing if he did not act when action became necessary for the fulfilment of his duty. Whatever the result of action he should calmly do his duty without seeking a reward.

Arjuna had the right and control over the action and not on its subsequent fruits. He emphasised that the action would have a greater effect if he put all his energy into it without being distracted by thinking of the result. Right action was bound to bring right result, so it was not necessary to run after it. Being successful in the path of action, he would become a Yogi and that would bring dignity to his life.

Shri Krishna told him that those who run after rewards lead a wretched life. A person with evenness of mind casts away both good and evil. He renounces the fruits of action and reaches the highest goal called

Moksha or liberation, which is free from all evil.

Listening to Shri Krishna, Arjuna asked him how to recognise such a man. A wise one, said Krishna, has full control over his desires and makes no demands on others for anything. He is calm in pain and pleasure He is neither too happy nor too sad. He accepts what happens without attachment or repulsion. He is not jealous of anybody. With a calm mind all his sorrows come to an end and he attains real peace of mind. Thus he becomes a man of discipline, having full control over his mind and body.

One who does not understand this, Shri Krishna continued, develops attachment to the senses from which spring desire. From desire comes anger and anger destroys reason, the intelligence to discriminate between right and wrong. Such a person loses happiness and peace of mind which comes to those who never think of 'I' and 'My' and thereby attain God and Nirvana.

The Way of Action

III

The man who rejoices in the Self, is satisfied with the Self and is content with the Self alone – he has nothing for which he should work.

Verse-19

Whatsoever a great man does, other men follow him and do the same. Whatever standard he sets up, is followed by most of the men in the world.

Verse-21

Listening to Shri Krishna, Arjuna was utterly perplexed. He was at a loss to know which was superior: knowledge or action. He asked Shri Krishna to clear up the apparent contradiction in His words and tell him the one way by which he could attain the highest good.

Shri Krishna explained that some men were suited to tread the path of knowledge and others to follow the path of action. Both existed side by side. No one could remain without action. Action was better than no action. Action was necessary even for maintenance of the body. Devotion to God, Shri Krishna said, was also action. Worship helped both God and man. He advised Arjuna to have trust in God and do his duty. This was also necessary because ordinary men followed the great in achieving the standard set by them.

Taking about Himself, Shri Krishna said that though He did not need anything, he kept on working. It was essential for the wise to show light to the unwise and encourage them to work along right lines.

Shri Krishna told Arjuna to have faith in Him and make himself ready to fight. He advised him to act, leaving the fruit of action to Him. The action should be selfless. The unwise did not see the value of selfless action and therefore suffered. He made it clear that we must play our part, great or small. One must do one's duty however distasteful it may be. One must be faithful to it unto death. Doing so even death brings blessedness.

Arjuna asked Shri Krishna why people committed sin against their will as if driven by an inner force. Shri Krishna replied that desire, anger and passion were at the root of all sins. They confused the mind and turned the wise into the unwise.

He advised Arjuna to conquer desire and thus acquire control over his senses. He added that greater than

the senses was the mind and greater
than the mind was the intellect. The
greatest of all was self-control,
attaining which one controlled all the
desires.

The Way of Knowledge

IV

I am born in every age for the protection of the good, for the destruction of the wicked and for the establishment of dharma.

Verse–8

As men approach Me, so do I seek them. All men follow My path from all sides.

Verse–77

Continuing the discourse, Shri Krishna told Arjuna that he imparted this Karma Yoga first of all to the Sun-god. This was long long ago. The Sun-god taught it to Manu, who handed it down the ages. With the passage of time this ancient wisdom was forgotten. He would now reveal it to Arjuna because He loved him, and considered him to be a friend.

Arjuna expressed surprise at Shri Krishna's statement that he had imparted the same wisdom to the Sun-god. He asked how this was possible since He was born only recently and the Sun was there since the beginning of creation.

Shri Krishna replied that Arjuna's question was reasonable because he did not know that both He (Krishna) and Arjuna had been born again and again though He knew about his earlier births and Arjuna did not. He explained, "You should know that I can take birth whenever I like. I come into the world whenever there is a decline of Truth (Dharma). It is My duty to save Dharma and I take birth for this great purpose. I always help and love My devotees. I do not mind the way they approach Me. They should have faith in Me to achieve salvation. Many have already achieved it. They can worship Me the way they like and obtain whatever they desire through action."

"Castes and creeds are created according to men's actions, and the qualities of their minds. They do their own duties. The whole world is bound by action. There is no life without action. The wise man acts but has no selfish desire in his mind. He does not care for the outcome of his actions. He is the same in success and failure, pain or pleasure, and is free from jealousy. He who has given up attachment to action and its fruit is always content. As he has subdued his mind and body and does no evil, he commits no sin and therefore experiences no guilt. He is happy under all circumstances and is free from birth and death."

Sacrifice was also an action, said Shri Krishna. One should be very careful while performing sacrificial rites. Sacrifices are offered in many ways. Some offer it to please the gods and goddesses. Some others offer it to be able to control their senses and attain self-realisation. There were also those who offer it in the name of Dharma and yet others who practise it to control their life and breath. Whatever the form of sacrifice, there is joy in it and all who perform it are praiseworthy.

Selfless action, however, was higher than all forms of sacrifice, Shri Krishna explained. Gaining of Knowledge could only be gained through reverence and serving of the Guru. Only the wise could teach the knowledge needed to understand the mysteries of God and self-discipline. Only through Knowledge could one understand the Atman and obtain peace of mind. The ignorant, having no faith, would not find happiness in this world or the next.

Shri Krishna urged Arjuna to resolve all his doubts through Knowledge and get ready to fight.

The Way of Renunciation

V

A person whose soul is no longer attached to the material objects finds the happiness that is in the Self. He whose heart is devoted to the contemplation of Brahma enjoys undying bliss.

Verse–21

The holy men whose sins are destroyed, whose doubts are dispelled, who have disciplined their minds and who devote themselves to the welfare of all beings attain God.

Verse–25

Arjuna was still undecided whether or not to fight. Shri Krishna had laid stress on renunciation of action and yet advised him to follow the path of action. Arjuna wanted to know which of the two was superior. He wanted an explanation in a language simple enough for him to understan 1.

Shri Krishna told Arjuna the Yoga of Knowledge and the Yoga of Action both lead to supreme bliss. However, the Yoga of Action is superior to the Yoga of Knowledge. It is also easier to practise. The Karmayogi through selfless action becomes a Sannyasi. The aim of the Sannyasi and the Karmayogi is the same and both attain salvation. The Karmayogi has the wisdom of the Sannyasi and is the master of his senses. He is like a lotus leaf unaffected by its surroundings. The Karmayogi always performs selfless action which results in self-purification. He always works without caring for the fruits of his actions. Such a Karmayogi obtains all Knowledge and realises that the Atman is not the doer of deeds. When he understands that it is nature that works and is the cause of attachment, he gives up the illusion that he is the doer, and comes nearer to God and is united with Him. When he reaches this stage he has the same respect for all, may they be wise or unwise, men or beasts. Such a person is blessed by God and is not affected by pain or pleasure. He is always happy and is not hurt by any circumstances. His source of happiness is his inner self and not external objects. As he is at peace with himself he commits no sin. Such a person has no desires or passions and is never angry and this gives him eternal bliss. He is the master of his senses, mind and intellect. He is friendly towards all and looks after their welfare. He is the soul of love and compassion and does good to all without expecting anything in return. He is not afraid of anything. Such a devotee attains peace.

The Way of Meditation

VI

He who looks on the pains and pleasures of all beings as he looks them in himself is a supreme person.

Verse–32

Mind is unsteady and difficult to curb but it can be controlled through practice of meditation and by warding off worldly ideas.

Verse–35

Shri Krishna, driving home his teaching about renunciation, told Arjuna that he who did his duty without expecting any reward was both a Sannyasi and a Yogi. There was no difference between them. They aimed to reach the same goal. They were like water which when filled in two different vessels remained the same. This was also true of Sannyasa and Yoga. No one who did not give up thoughts of the world could become a Yogi. The path of duty was the only ladder by which one could reach the highest Yoga.

Shri Krishna then told Arjuna about the power of the Self. He said one should lift oneself up by one's own efforts. A man is his own friend and enemy. He who has realised his real self is perfectly at ease in all circumstances. He is at peace in heat and cold, joy and sorrow, honour and dishonour. He is equally at ease amidst proverty and riches. His calm and serenity are not disturbed. He who regards friends and foes, the virtuous and the sinner, alike stands supreme.

Shri Krishna then told Arjuna how a Yogi should train himself for meditation. The Yogi should choose a place of solitude and a seat which is neither too high nor too low. He should have complete control over his mind and senses. Holding his body, head and neck straight, he should look at the tip of his nose. (This Yogic posture is a well known aid to concentration).

With his mind focussed on Him, said Shri Krishna, he will find himself at peace and attain supreme bliss. A true Yogi does not go to extremes. He performs his duties, is never in sorrow. He has control over himself and his desires and does not waver in his efforts. He experiences true joy and happiness through the intellect. To him meditation is a joy — the joy of an enlightened man. There are still many obstacles in his way but he is not shaken. Through self-control he subdues his mind and obtains peace. This brings him the highest happiness and supreme bliss. Such a person sees God in all living beings and becomes the most accomplished Yogi, remaining equally calm in pain and pleasure.

Knowing that it is most difficult to gain control over the ever wavering mind, Arjuna asked Shri Krishna how he could achieve mastery over it. Shri Krishna replied that this was indeed a difficult task. He asserted that the mind could be tamed through self-control, ceaseless effort, concentration and dedication.

Arjuna next asked Shri Krishna what happened to one who, though having faith, could not subdue his passions and control his mind. Without waiting for an answer, he said such a person would experience neither worldly pleasures nor heavenly bliss. He wanted Shri Krishna to tell him what the fate of such a person would be. He and only He could clear his doubts.

Shri Krishna's reply was reassuring. He told Arjuna that sincere efforts and actions were never wasted. A good man could never meet with an evil end. He went to a pla   7

for the good and was rebo

world in a noble family wh

was held in high esteem, peop   e

god-fearing, had regard for truth and were learned scholars. Here in this place he pursued his practice with great vigour and strived further for perfection. Through continued meditation and concentration he reached the supreme state.

Shri Krishna advised Arjuna to become a Yogi as a Yogi was superior to both the man of knowledge and the ascetic. He realises the unity of man and God. Of all the Yogis he who worships Him is the greatest. A great gi was a great devotee also. The relationship between Him and the Yogi could only be compared to that between the body and the soul.

The Way of Realisation

VII

Four types of virtuous men worship me. They are–the man in distress, the man seeking knowledge, the man seeing enjoyment and the man endowed with wisdom.

Verse–16

I confer on the devotee unflinching faith on whichever image of form he chooses to worship.

Verse–21

Shri Krishna told Arjuna He would teach him in full how to experience true knowledge of the divine. Out of thousands of men only a few strove for it and among them only the rare ones reached the goal.

Earth, water, fire, air and ether and the mind, intellect and ego, explained Shri Krishna, comprise the lower nature. The higher nature which sustains the whole world is Atman. It is revealed in both higher and lower forms. The whole world rests on this energy. There is nothing in the world which is superior to Him and nothing exists without Him.

Continuing His discourse, He clarified that He is supreme and is at the core of everything. He is the wisdom of the wise. He is the strength of the strong and is free from desires and passions. He explained that whatever there is of the nature of *Sattva*, *Rajas* and *Tamas* — the spiritual, the earthly and the base — originated from Him but He is not in them. It is very hard to overcome them. Only through knowledge could this be done. The evil-doers who are foolish and deprived of knowledge do not understand Him. Shri Krishna then described the four types of men who wanted to acquire true knowledge.

They are– the man in distress, the man seeking knowledge, the man seeking enjoyment, and the man endowed with wisdom. Of them the man of knowledge, of single-minded devotion, is most dear to Him. Such men are the incarnation of divinity and reach that state after several births. He said many worship Him through other gods and goddesses. If they worship with full faith, He fulfils their wishes. But as He is the Supreme God, those who are devoted to Him in body, mind and soul received the supreme bliss.

He told Arjuna that the unwise thought of Him in human forms and did not know His supreme nature. He is beyond birth and death and knows everything about the past, the present and the future. This is not understood by the ordinary people who were ignorant. Only men of virtuous deeds who live and work with love and serve their fellowmen can know Him. Only they can have the real knowledge. Only the hearts of the wise can unite with Him.

The Way to the Indestructible Brahma

VIII

Therefore, at all times remember Me only and fight with mind and intellect focussed on Me; you shall certainly come to Me alone.

Verse–7

I am easily accessible to that ever steadfast Yogi who constantly meditates on Me and gives no thought to anything else.

Verse–14

Arjuna, not quite understanding what Shri Krishna had said about Brahma, the individual soul, Atman, and action, wanted to know more about these realities.

Shri Krishna, answering Arjuna's questions, said Brahma is supreme and indestructible and as Atman resides in all beings. Brahma is all powerful, is present everywhere and knows everything. One should glorify Him at all times, even when leaving the world. One who at the time of death thinks of God, is united with Him; whatever a man thinks of at the final moment that he becomes, for that is the thought uppermost in his mind.

Shri Krishna reminded Arjuna of his immediate duty, which was to fight. One who performs his duty in the spirit of a Karmayogi attains supreme bliss. The way to reach it is to firmly believe in God and meditate on the word 'OM' and go on doing it. This is the only way to salva.ion. Such a Yogi is released from the cycle of life and death. He reaches the pure Brahma and attains the highest bliss. All others are reborn again and again.

Explaining further, Shri Krishna said Brahma's days and nights are of a long duration. In the course of a day and night of the Brahma comes about the beginning and end of the world, and this cycle goes on. He told Arjuna that Brahma is eternal, indestructible. Brahma is not destroyed when the universe is destroyed.

Brahma does not perish with the end of beings. The Imperishable Great Unknown is called the supreme destination. This is God's abode from which there is no return. There is no rebirth for those who have attained Him. The supreme destination can be attained only through undivided devotion.

Talking further about life and death, Shri Krishna said some come to the end of life while on the path of light. They experience Brahma. This leads them on the straight path of salvation. There are others who die when there is darkness all around. There is no salvation for them. They are reborn. These two paths are eternal and the Yogi knowing them attains the supreme eternal state through steady discipline.

The Way of Royal Knowledge and Royal Mystery

IX

Whatever you do, whatever you eat, whatever you offer in sacrifice, whatever you give and whatever austerities you practise, do it as an offering to Me.

Verse–27

All persons, even of low classes, who take refuge in Me, also attain the highest goal.

Verse–32

Shri Krishna told Arjuna He would reveal to him the great secret which is at the root of all wisdom. He would, in simple language, describe the mystery of knowledge of Brahma and the world. This ultimate wisdom brings joy and happiness to the seeker. It is within ourselves and can be acquired without much difficulty. It is perceived by direct experience, is in accord with righteousness and is imperishable.

Shri Krishna explained that He is the cause of creation of this universe. He brings all beings into existence and sustains them. It is under His control that nature gives birth to all. Though he is within all beings, He is indifferent to their activities and remains unattached. This is the great doctrine. He is everywhere and He is nowhere.

Those who have faith in Him, Shri Krishna continued, are released from the endless cycle of life and death. They are the really wise people. But the foolish ones, not knowing His true glory, waste their lives away. The wise know Him in every form. For them there is no distinction between the rich and the poor, between the small and the great and they radiate joy to all. They have no pride and show courtesy to one and all. There is harmony in their internal feelings and external behaviour.

Knowing Him to be the source of all beings, Shri Krishna continued, the wise worship Him with their minds focussed on Him. They forever glorify Him and are steadfast in their single-minded devotion. There are others who worship Him in many other ways.

Shri Krishna told Arjuna He was there, centre of all offerings, and identifies Himself with the sacrifice and so with Brahma. He is the father of the whole universe and the guardian of all creation. He is the giver and the defender of all life and is the supporter of the universe. He is also the cause of all destruction. By His will alone everything meets its end. In short, He is the root cause of its birth, sustenance and death.

Shri Krishna said He fulfils the wishes of all his devotees. He removes all their anxieties and helps them in achieving what they want. He even sends them to heaven if they wish. But having enjoyed their stay there, they return to the world of the mortals. Only the true believers are freed from the cycle of life and death.

Talking about His devotees, Shri Krishna made it clear to Arjuna that He makes no distinction between the great and the small. He accepts the worship of every devotee. The true means of attaining Him is simply through pure devotion and love. Superiority of birth, excellence of race, age or beauty do not matter. Without devotion everything is useless. He advises Arjuna to surrender all his actions to Him and feel relieved of his burden. It is the only way to attain happiness. It is the simplest method of Yoga. No time should be wasted in performing the formalities. He is always with his devotees. Even the sinners are saved through worship. The religion of love is open to all. All receive equal love from Him.

Shri Krishna said his devotees are never destroyed, and achieve everlasting peace. He advises Arjuna to worship Him with his body and soul. This is the great secret by realising which he will secure true happiness.

The Way of Divine Perfections

X

I am the Self, seated in the hearts of all beings. I am the beginning, the middle and the end of all beings.

Verse–20

Whatever glorious or beautiful or mighty beings that exist anywhere, know that it was sprung from a spark of My splendour.

Verse–41

Shri Krishna told Arjuna that He would repeat what He had said before because it pleased Him to do so, and because it was for his benefit and welfare.

Shri Krishna said that He is the creator of the whole universe and the primary source of all life. Just as light and darkness are produced by the same Sun, so He is the cause of all pain and pleasure, happiness and misery, fame and ill fame, fear and courage, life and death.

He is the master of the universe and all the great saints and seers came to know Him through worship, love and devotion. This is the only way to dispel the darkness born of ignorance. This is the only way to experience supreme happiness and achieve the highest goal.

Listening to Shri Krishna, Arjuna said he was thoroughly convinced of the truth of every word He had said. Never before had he realised the greatness of His qualities and wanted to know more about the entire range of His divine powers and manifestations Arjun wanted to hear, again and again, about the forms He had assumed. Arjuna said that His discourse was supreme nectar and he wanted more of it. Shri Krishna told Arjuna that He had assumed countless forms. Just as no one could count the number of hair on his body or the drops of water when it rained, so He was unable to tell him about all His forms. He could talk only about the pre-eminent ones.

Shri Krishna said He is limitless and is the soul of every living being. He is the beginning, the middle and the end of all that lives. Of the heavenly deities, He is Krishna, the chief one. Of the shining objects He is the Sun with rays of wonderful light. Of the planets in the sky, He is the Moon. He is Indra, the first of the Vedic gods, and He is Samaveda, the first among the Vedas. He is the mind among the senses and the life force among the living beings. He is Shiva. He is Meru, the highest among the towering mountains. He is the ocean, He is Brighu, the sacred Himalaya, Narada. He is the nectar, the supreme among the liquids; He is the king of all kings. He is Varuna, the water deity. He is Yama and Dharma who are witnesses to all good and bad actions of living beings and reward them according to their deeds. He is the lion, the eagle, the wind, the Ganga and the crocodile. He is Rama, the great warrior. He is the Gayatri Mantra, He is the vowel 'अ' (a) and the syllable 'OM'.

Shri Krishna told Arjuna it was impossible to speak of all his manifestations. He had described some of them, What was the need of telling him about them all? It was enough that He is the seed from which all human beings are born and that He is the creator of the universe.

So Shri Krishna advised Arjuna not to make any distinction between the rich and the poor, the high and the low. To do so was a great error.

The Vision of the Universal Form

XI

Therefore, stand up and win glory, conquer your enemies and enjoy a prosperous kingdom. They have already been killed by Me, you be only the instrument.

Verse-33

He who does all actions for Me, who looks upon Me as the supreme goal, who is devoted to Me, who is free from attachment, and he who hates nobody and bears enmity to none — he comes to Me.

Verse-55

Arjuna thanked Shri Krishna for revealing to him the mystery of the Self. It had helped him, he said, in clearing his mental fog and in understanding the origin and the end of all beings. He was now eager to see with his own eyes Shri Krishna's universal and imperishable form.

Shri Krishna agreed to fulfil Arjuna's desire. He said He was a limitless mass of forms. There were many forms He assumed which none had seen before. They were of diverse hues and shapes. Arjuna could see the whole universe in Him. To enable him to do so, Shri Krishna gave Arjuna the divine eye.

What a sight! Arjuna beheld Shri Krishna's countless forms. Innumerable faces appeared before him. He saw the marvel of the whole universe: one wonder after another. Arjuna was happy that his great ambition had been fulfilled and his heart experienced immense peace.

Arjuna said he could see in Him the diverse hosts of beings — all the gods, the seers, sages and celestial beings. He could see endless forms without knowing their beginning, middle or the end. He could see the lustre surrounding Him. He beheld Shri Krishna as the Lord of the whole universe: Indestructible, Eternal,

Imperishable, possessing unlimited powers, having full control over heaven and hell. He could see the gods paying Him respect and praising His glory. Arjuna could also see the demons and all lower beings trembling at the sight of his limitless forms, overcome with awe.

Arjuna confessed that after seeing those terrible sights he was completely shaken. He saw a huge fire coming out of His mouth dragging both the Kauravas and the Pandavas. He said they were being swallowed, crushed in his teeth, wholly destroyed.

Seeing His frightful form, Arjuna said he had lost the peace of his mind.

He asked Shri Krishna who He was that assumed this awesome form, why He did it and why He was bent upon the destruction he saw.

Shri Krishna told Arjuna that the form was Death in person. He reminded him that he had already seen the Kaurava and the Pandava armies dying. In fact the life in them had already been destroyed. Arjuna had only to kill them and take the credit for having done so. He had only to fight and be victorious.

Greatly stirred by listening to what Shri Krishna had told him, Arjuna bowed down his head and stood there with folded hands. Kneeling before

Him he told Shri Krishna that He was the Supreme Being and it was natural that the whole universe was filled with His love and, praising His glory, paid Him homage. He was imperishable and the greatest of the great. He was the creator of the universe and the hope of all mankind.

Arjuna begged Shri Krishna to be forgiven for any lack of respect on his part. He requested him to accept his prayer as He was the greatest of all teachers. He told Shri Krishna that it was at his own request that Krishna had shown him His universal form. He, however, could not endure this unique vision any longer and was frightened and terrified. He said he was longing to see Him in His original form, be near Him, and talk to Him.

Shri Krishna told Arjuna that no one had ever seen what he had seen. He knew what no one had ever known before. No one had even achieved the power to see what he had seen.

Arjuna was very fortunate to have witnessed Shri Krishna's universal form. Shri Krishna asked Arjuna to shed all fear, and feelings of weakness, that the rare experience of seeing His true self might have roused in him.

Saying this Shri Krishna transformed Himself into His original form and comforted the terrified Pandava.

Seeing Him in the human form Arjuna's confidence was restored and he felt calm and composed.

Shri Krishna told Arjuna that even the gods pined to see His Vishwarupa — Universal Form. Neither through knowledge, renunciation nor charity could anybody see what he had seen. The knowledge of God and union with Him could be had only through undivided love and complete devotion. He who gave up hatred of all beings, had malice towards none, and loved alike all creatures, high and low, rich and poor, reached Him.

The Way of Divine Love

XII

Knowledge is better than practice, meditation is better than knowledge, renunciation of the fruits of action is better than meditation, peace immediately follows such renunciation.

Verse–12

He to whom honour and dishonour are equal, who is silent, content with whatever he has, has no fixed home to live, has a firm mind and is full of devotion—that man is dear to Me.

Verse–19

Shri Krishna had talked about the path of devotion and the path of Yoga. Arjuna wanted to know which was the better of the two. He asked Shri Krishna to explain to him who was more dear to Him, the devotee who followed the path of devotion or one who pursued the path of Yoga.

Shri Krishna replied that his best devotee was one who was steadfast in his faith in Him and worshipped Him with deep concentration. But the seekers of wisdom were also His devotees. They sought to control their passions and their senses through rigid discipline. They had equipoise of mind and were dedicated to the welfare of all beings. Of course, their task was much more difficult.

Shri Krishna explained that those on the path of devotion had their hearts turned towards Him. They did so with single-minded concentration with body, speech and mind. Their mind always fixed on Him, they attained the fulfilment of their aim.

What should they do if they were unable to fix their mind on Him? Constant practice, said Shri Krishna, is the remedy for them. If this was also not possible they should seek to reach Him through work. But no wrong should be done and all work should be dedicated to Him without ever thinking that 'I' am doing this.

If the mind does not have the firmness to do this, Shri Krishna continued, then they should practise control of the senses, and renounce the fruit of all action. The performance of action without desire appears very simple but it is the highest Yoga. To sum up, said Shri Krishna, knowledge was better than the practice of concentration, meditation excelled knowledge and renunciation of the fruit of action was even superior to meditation. It led to supreme happiness and peace.

Shri Krishna explained that his devotees did not hate anyone; they were friendly to all, free from egoism and were even-minded in pain and pleasure. They were by nature forgiving, were ever content and, with firm conviction of mind and vision, were devoted to Him. They had the highest love for Him.

His devotees, continued Shri Krishna, were not a source of trouble to the world. They were fearless and free from joy and anger. They were neither perturbed nor afraid. They were free from longing and craved for nothing. They were pure, impartial and competent. Things of the world did not distract their minds and they were indifferent o the fruits of action. They neither rejoiced nor grieved. They did not hate anybody and had no desires. They were the same in joy and sorrow. They were beyond good and evil and were full of devotion to Him.

His devotees, Shri Krishna added, had the same feelings, for friends and foes, the same attitude towards honour and dishonour, pleasure and pain. They were the same in heat and in cold. In short, they were free from all attachment. They were not affected by censure or praise and were fully content with whatever came their way and whatever they possessed. They had calmness of mind.

Those who followed the path of wisdom with full faith and were solely devoted to Him, said Shri Krishna, were very dear to Him.

Discrimination between the Body and the Soul

XIII

Constancy in the knowledge of the Self, an insight into the object of the knowledge of truth — this is declared to be true knowledge and all that is contrary to it is ignorance.

Verse–11

As only one sun illumines the whole world, so does He who dwells in the body illumines the whole body.

Verse–33

Arjuna now sought to know what is the body and who is the knower of the body, and who is its controller and protector.

Shri Krishna told him the body was the Field and he was the knower of all fields and was their protector. He said He would make him understand, in a nutshell, all that he wanted to know about the Field and about His powers.

Shri Krishna said real knowledge lay in humility, non-violence, tolerance, simplicity, self-control and steadfastness. Preception of birth, death, old age and disease, non-attachment to children, the family and home, and peace of mind in favourable and unfavourable circumstances, meditation in solitude and understanding of the Self, the Atman, the God. This is the real knowledge and anything contrary to it is ignorance.

He told Arjuna He would now speak to him at length about the supreme Brahma: God who is beyond cause and effect, from whom all life emerges. He is devoid of all senses, yet shines through them. He is inside and outside all beings, and though far away is very near. God has form and is also formless. He resides in every heart. This was the wide field of God.

Nature and Spirit, Shri Krishna said, are both eternal. Nature is the cause of all material activities and effects and Spirit is the cause of the experience of all sufferings and enjoyments through the physical body. Nature is the cause of all life and death, yet the individual is part of God. He who thus knows Spirit and Nature along with its threefold qualities is not born again, however, he may conduct himself. Some perceived the Self through meditation, some through worship and some others through selfless action or Karmayoga. There are also those who do not know these means and hear about the Self from others. They also pass beyond death.

Shri Krishna told Arjuna that if he had followed all that had been explained to him it would be easy for him to understand that whatever object, animate or inanimate, is produced, it is through the union of the Field and the knower of the Field. God is the only reality as it abides in all beings. He does not perish when they perish. He who sees God abiding alike everywhere and does not kill this self by the Self, reaches the supreme state. He sees that work is done only through nature and realises that he is not the doer. He who perceives that the diverse existence of all beings is centred in One and that all evolution is from that One, alone attains Brahma. This imperishable supreme self though dwelling in the body neither acts nor is stained by action. It is like the ether that pervades all things, but is not stained by them because of its subtle character. The Self within everything illumines them as the sun illumines the whole world.

Discrimination between the mortal body and the immortal soul, Brahma, Atman, is the most important knowledge that man can acquire. And when he comes to understand that nothing can be achieved without the help of God, a close and permanent relationship is established between mortal man and the immortal God within him, and when he reaches this stage, he achieves his life's purpose, the realisation of the divine within himself and in the universe.

Discriminations of the Three *Gunas*

XIV

Sattva attaches to happiness, *Rajas* to action, while *Tamas* veils knowledge and binds one to helplessness.

Verse–9

He who serves Me with intense, unswerving devotion transcends the lord of the three *Gunas*, and becomes fit to be one with Brahma.

Verse–26

Shri Krishna, elaborating on the supreme wisdom by gaining which all the sages had attained the highest perfection, said the knowledge of the Self is above everything else. It is through the knowledge of the Self that one is released from the bond of birth and death and becomes one with Him. The whole world was created by His association with Nature, so he was called the father and Nature was called the mother; the universe was the child.

There are, Shri Krishna said, three *Gunas* — natural traits which exist, in small or large measure, in all human beings. They are *Sattva*, *Rajas* and

Tamas. *Sattva* is supreme, *Rajas* is the middling and *Tamas* the lowest.

Sattva is illuminating. It ties the soul in bonds of happiness and wisdom. It gives peace and enlightenment.

Rajas is born of passion and desire. It causes attachment to work and actions and their fruits.

Tamas is born of ignorance. It confuses the mind, causes blunders and generates sloth and indolence.

In short, *Sattva* urges one to happiness, *Rajas* to action and *Tamas* to negligence. Each *Guna* asserts itself by prevailing over the other *Gunas* and overshadows them. When *Sattva* is predominant, there is happiness and goodness among the people. When *Rajas* is in the ascendant, there is attraction to worldly activities and performance of work with selfish motives. *Rajas* is marked by intense physical activity. With the growth of *Tamas*, the mind and senses are clouded with darkness, resulting in laziness and carelessness.

Shri Krishna explained that when, at the time of one's death *Sattva* prevails, one goes to heaven where all men of noble deeds go; when *Rajas* is dominant one is born among those attached to action, and when *Tamas* is uppermost, one is born among stupid persons.

The fruit of *Sattvic* action is happiness and wisdom, the fruit of *Rajasic* action is sorrow and that of *Tamas* is ignorance. From *Sattva* comes knowledge, from *Rajas* greed and from *Tamas* ignorance. Those who abide in goodness go upward, the passionate stand in the middle and the base go downward.

The sage is beyond the *Gunas*. He is able to transcend them and being free from birth and death becomes immortal.

Arjuna asked Shri Krishna how to recognise the man who had risen above the *Gunas*. How did he behave and how did he transcend the *Gunas*?

Shri Krishna said such a man is unconcerned with and uninfluenced by the *Gunas*. He remains indifferent to them. He regards alike happiness and misery. He considers stone and a piece of gold of equal worth. Praise and blame, honour and insult, good and bad things make no difference to him. He has the same attitude to friends and foes. He does not look forward to the fruits of his actions. Such a person transcends the effect of the three *Gunas*. One should watch the *Gunas* in one's character, eradicate *Tamas*, control *Rajas* and, when *Sattva* predominates, beware of pride and the ego. This is the precious knowledge.

Shri Krishna said such grace could be achieved through dedication and devotion to Him and such a person merges in Brahma which is immortal, imperishable, eternal.

The Way to the Supreme Self

XV

The light that is in the sun and illumines the whole universe, the light that is in the moon and is likewise in fire — know that light to be Mine.

Verse-12

And I am seated in the hearts of all; from Me are memory and knowledge as well as their absence. It is I alone who is to be known through all the Vedas. I am indeed the author of Vedanta and the knower of the Vedas.

Verse-15

Shri Krishna, further explaining His true nature, told Arjuna that the universe is like a tree. So is worldly life. The shoots of the branches are the objects of the senses. The tree, right from the roots to the branches, is unreal, and so are the actions of man and the fruits of his actions. The senses can be controlled through wisdom and renunciation by turning away from all objects of worldly enjoyment. One should realise His true self which has no form and no attributes. This is the ultimate goal, the supreme state, which can be attained by those who shed pride and delusion, who have conquered the evil of attachment and who have controlled their desires and are not affected by pleasure and pain. Having reached this state they attain unity in Me and for them the cycle of birth and death ends.

Then, Shri Krishna continued, there is the soul which is present in each time. The soul is reborn according to the actions of the body. The soul remains the soul; action and enjoyment belong to the body. The power of the soul is eternal. Only the learned and Yogis know that in the soul there is no action. Only they understand the Atman and see it in themselves.

Shri Krishna went on to explain His glory to Arjuna. He told him that He is the supreme spirit. He is the brilliance in the sun, the moon and the fire. He dispels the darkness of the universe. He sustains the planets and all the beings living on them. He is the source of all energy and nourishes all plant life. He is the pulsation of life in every living being and sustains it through food needed by him. He is seated in the hearts of all and is the source of all wisdom and reason, the author of Vedanta and the knower of the Vedas.

There are two modes of being, continued Shri Krishna, the perishable and the imperishable. The material incarnation is perishable and the spiritual imperishable. In other words, the body is mortal and the soul immortal. He is superior to both body and soul. He is the prime immortal force and is, therefore, known as Purushottama, the supreme person. The wise know Him by this name and worship Him by this name.

Shri Krishna told Arjuna that He had given Him the most profound knowledge acquiring which a person becomes wise and perfect.

The Divine and the Demoniac

XVI

He who discards the injunctions of the scriptures and act upon the impulse of the desires attains neither perfection nor happiness, nor the highest goal.

Verse–23

Therefore let the scriptures be your authority for determining what should be done and what should not be done. You should do your work in the world according to the rules of the sciptures.

Verse–24

Shri Krishna, continuing his discourse, told Arjuna that there are two types of people born in this world. They are the divine and the demoniac. First of all, He described the virtues of the divine which enable them to attain wisdom. These are: Fearlessness, Intelligence, Wisdom, Charity, Self-control, Non-violence Truthfulness, Freedom from anger, Renunciation, Peaceful disposition, Compassion, Kindness, Non-attachment, Gentleness, Sense of shame, Forgiveness, Steadfastness, Purity of thought, Freedom from hatred, Humility, Austerity, Absence of greed, Study of scriptures (Vedas), Uprightness, and Sacrifice.

The vices of the demoniac, Shri Krishna said, are: Hypocrisy, Pride, Arrogance, Anger, Harshness and Ignorance. These constitute obstacles to the path of liberation and cause worldly troubles, unlike the divine virtues which set one free. He told Arjuna that he should not be afraid because he had all the divine virtues.

Shri Krishna explained that persons of demoniac nature do not know what to do and what not to do. They are not clear and pure in body and mind. They do not believe in truth and do not know how to behave. They feel the world is unreal, without any foundation and without any God. They feel that the world is brought about by the force of desire and lust. Such persons, having no intelligence, engage themselves in activities which lead to the destruction of the world. They are proud, arrogant and have false prestige and insatiable lust. They engage themselves in action with impure intentions.

The demoniac, continued Shri Krishna, give themselves to the enjoyment of sensuous pleasures all their lives and feel that this is the real joy of life. They are driven by hundreds of desires, lust and anger and acquire wealth by illegal means. They do so for the gratification of their lust. Such rich fools always think of their wealth, and plan ways and means of acquiring more for the enjoyment of pleasures of all kinds. All the time, they boast of having killed their enemies and are always planning to kill anyone who defies them. They feel that they are perfect, powerful and happy. They feel that with all their wealth they have become men of great status. They think that by donating some money in charity they will become the happiest of men. Such ignorant people, having all sorts of wrong thoughts, give in to all types of sensuous pleasure, go to hell: standing in the way of real human progress.

Shri Krishna said the demoniac, influenced by their own importance, and self-praise, full of intoxication of wealth and honour, perform sacrifices which are only in name.

Such persons possess false ego, vanity, pride, lust and anger and become envious of the supreme personality which is situated in their own bodies and in others. Such persons are evil, cruel, hateful, wicked and are thrown back into the ocean of degraded species because of their envious and mischievous behaviour. Such foolish people are born again and again; can never attain salvation and gradually sink down to the lowest state of existence.

Lust, anger and greed, Shri Krishna said, are the three gates leading to hell. They are the three fountain-heads of misery. They destroy the good in man. Every sane person should shun them. Such a person works his own salvation and thereby reaches the highest goal.

A person who does not care for the wisdom given in the scriptures and the duties prescribed therein attains neither perfection, nor happiness, nor the highest goal.

Shri Krishna advised Arjuna to act according to the instructions given in the scriptures. The teaching of the Shastras are not unreal. They should be accepted. Arjuna should know what should be done and what should not be done. He should act on the lines laid down by the sages and this will set an example for others to follow.

The Threefold Faith

XVII

The faith of every individual is in accordance with his nature. A man is made of his faith, he is what his faith is.

Verse-3

Whatever sacrifice or gift is made, whatever austerity is practised, whatever ceremony is observed, if it is done without faith, it is called *asat* or 'unreal'. It is of no account here or hereafter.

Verse-28

Shri Krishna, explaining the nature of men's faith, told Arjuna that it was of three kinds. It corresponds to their natural desposition and is characterised by the *Gunas*. Faith constitutes the very being of a man: he is whatever the nature of his faith is. Faith is the main support of life.

Men of a *Sattvic* disposition, said Shri Krishna, worship the gods, those of a *Rajasic* temperament worship the demons and those of a *Tamasic* outlook worship the spirits and ghosts. There are persons who do not care for the scriptures and flout the rules given therein. Theirs is false worship, coloured by egoism, hypocrisy, passion, violence and desire. They come to grief. They only torture their bodies and souls.

Continuing, Shri Krishna said that sacrifice, austerity and charity are also of three kinds. They differ according to the three modes of nature.

Men of a *Sattvic* disposition like foods which promote longevity, intelligence, strength, health, happiness and satisfaction. Such foods are sweet, nourishing and tasty. People endowed with *Rajas* favour foods which are bitter, acidic, salted and very hot. Such foods cause pain, illness and misery.

People endowed with *Tamas* like food which is ill cooked, stale, insipid and polluted. Such food hurts the stomach and other organs. It stimulates base desires and lust which lead to a sinful life.

Sattvic sacrifice is that which is performed according to the scriptural rules. It is offered as a matter of duty without desire for any reward.

Rajasic sacrifice is performed for material gain and reputation. Hypocrisy is at the back of such sacrifice.

Tamasic sacrifice, offered not in accordance with the scriptural rules and in which there is no chanting of hymns, no distribution of food, no *Dakshana* (donation with due respect) to priests, is devoid of faith.

Austerity, Shri Krishna explained, is also of three kinds: in body, mind and spirit. There are three categories: corporal, literary and mental.

Austerity of the body comprises worship of God, Brahman, teachers and the wise, cleanliness, simplicity, celibacy and non-violence.

Austerity of speech consists in speaking what is truthful and beneficial to others and causes no agitation to them. Also it is in the study and recitation of the Vedas.

Austerity of the mind, Shri Krishna explained, constitutes cheerfulness, sincerity, control and purity of heart. *Sattvic* austerity is observed without any expectations of material gain and for the sake of goodness of heart.

Rajasic austerity is observed with the expectation of gaining respect, honour and pride and is for show. Its outcome is uncertain and transitory.

Tamasic austerity is practised with a determination based on foolishness. It tortures the self and harms others.

Charity, Shri Krishna added, has also a threefold division. The best kind of charity is that which is given to a worthy person at a proper place and time. It is given as a matter of duty without any consideration of return or benefit to oneself. It is called charity of a *Sattvic* mode and is for divine love.

Charity given for the sake of deriving some benefit in return and done in a grudging manner is of *Tamasic* nature. It is a gift made to an underserving person at an improper time and place.

Brahma, said Shri Krishna, has also a threefold designation: *Om Tat Sat*. By means of it were created the Brahmins, the Vedas and the sacrifices. These holy words indicate the Supreme Absolute Truth. They are used by the Brahmins while chanting the hymns

of the Vedas and performing sacrifices
and ceremonies.

All acts of sacrifice, austerity and
charity are always begun with the
utterance of *Om*. With the utterance
of *Tat* and without desiring any
reward these various acts are
performed by those seeking liberation.
Sat is used in the sense of a
praiseworthy act, truth and goodness.
Steadfastness in sacrifice, austerity
and charity is also designated as *Sat*
and so also any action connected with
it. So all deeds performed in the faith
of God are acts of piety.

All acts of sacrifice, austerity and
charity and any other action

performed without faith are called *asat*. Such actions are of no help in this life or the next.

Deliverance through Renunciation

Control of mind, control of the senses, undergoing hardship for the sake of duty, internal and external purity, forgiveness, straightness of mind and belief in God are the qualities of a noble soul.

Verse–42

Fix your heart on Me, give your love to Me, worship Me, bow down before Me, so shall you come to Me. This is my pledge to you, for you are dear to Me.

Verse–65

This chapter sums up all that has been said before.

. Arjuna now requested Shri Krishna to explain to him the fine distinction in the meanings of renunciation and non-attachment: *Sannyasa* and *Tyaga*.

Shri Krishna replied that abandonment of all action is called renunciation — *Sannyasa,* and the abandonment of the fruits of action is called non-attachment — *Tyaga*.

There are three kinds of renunciation. Some wise men feel that all work should be given up while others think that exceptions must be made in the case of works of sacrifice, austerity and charity. These must continue to be practised in all circumstances as they purify the heart. But acts of sacrifice, austerity and charity and all other duties, said Shri Krishna, must be performed without any expectation of reward.

Non-attachment, inspired by base desires, is said to be of the nature of *Tamas*, continued Shri Krishna. Non-attachment arising from the fear of physical suffering is said to be of the nature of *Rajas*. Non-attachment born of proper understanding and without hope of any reward is said to be characterised by *Sattva*. A man of true renunciation will neither do any unpleasant work nor cling to a pleasant one.

Bearing a body itself signifies that work can never be abandoned entirely. But a true renouncer is one who renounces the fruits of action.

The fruit of works, Shri Krishna said, is threefold — good, evil and mixed. It accrues to those who have not renounced, but none to the non-attached.

There are five causes that bring about the accomplishment of a work. These are: the body, the doer (*Jivatma*), the senses, the functions of the vital breaths, and destiny.

There are five causes of action which a man undertakes with his body, speech or mind, be it right or wrong. He who has a false ego and thinks he is the doer is without any intellect. But he who is free from egoism and whose intellect is not stained, even if he kills is not a killer. He is not bound by his deeds.

The three incentives for action are: knowledge, object of knowledge and the knower. All work is accomplished through three factors: the senses, the object and the doer. Knowledge, work and the doer are also threefold depending on the three *Gunas*.

Sattvic knowledge is that through which a man sees the one imperishable entity that exists in all the beings.

Rajasic knowledge is that through which one clings to a single individual as if he were all and thinks that there exists nothing beyond the body.

Action performed in accordance with the scriptures without love and hatred and with no desire for fruit is *Sattvic*. Action done under the influence of the false ego, which involves strain and is undertaken for the sake of enjoyment, is *Rajasic*.

Action undertaken through ignorance, without thinking of one's capacity and meant to injure others is *Tamasic*.

One who performs work without the false ego, caring for neither success nor failure, and with enthusiasm and without any attachment is said to be of a *Sattvic* nature.

The doer who is passionate and greedy, is given to violence, is affected by joy and sorrow, is attached to work and the fruit thereof is said to be of a *Rajasic* nature.

The doer who lacks self-control, is arrogant, proud and is a cheat, depriving others of their livelihood is said to be of a *Tamasic* nature.

Shri Krishna, continuing, told Arjuna that discipline and intellect are also of three kind and are related to the three *Gunas*.

The intellect which understands right action and inaction and can differentiate between work that should be done and work that should not be done, between fear and fearlessness, and between bondage and liberation, is *Sattvic*.

The intellect which cannot understand what is right and what is wrong and decide which work should be done and which work should not be done is *Rajasic*.

The intellect which is envolved in ignorance and regards wrong to be right is *Tamasic*.

The discipline with which one holds firm the activities of the mind, the breath and the senses through Yoga is *Sattvic*.

The discipline with which one holds fast virtue, wealth and pleasure seeking the fruit of action with intense attachment is *Rajasic*.

The firmess with which one does not give up sleep, fear, sorrow, elation, despair or arrogance is *Tamasic*.

Shri Krishna told Arjuna that happiness is also of three kinds.

That which is like poison in the beginning but nectar in the end and which comes from the bliss of self-realisation is *Sattvic*.

The happiness that is born out of desire and appears to be nectar in the beginning but in the end is like poison is *Rajasic*.

The happiness which deadens the soul both in the beginning and in the end and which is derived from sleep, carelessness and laziness is *Tamasic*.

Continuing, Shri Krishna said all actions by men and gods are influenced by the three *Gunas*. The duties of Brahmins, Kshatriyas, Vaisyas and Sudras are assigned according to these *Gunas*.

Peacefulness, self-control, austerity, purity, tolerance, honesty, wisdom, knowledge and piety are the qualities of a Brahmin.

Heroism, majesty, determination, skill and courage in battle, generousity and leadership are the qualities of a Kshatriya.

Agriculture, cattle-rearing and trade are the duties of a Vaisya.

Service of all, through hard work and labour is the duty of a Sudra.

Shri Krishna told Arjuna that a man devoted to his own duty according to God's will attains perfection. By following one's own Dharma one can know what one's duty is. Whatever the circumstances one should attend to one's duty.

He whose mind is not attached to anything, who has subdued his self and is free from all desires reaches the highest perfection and attains freedom from action.

He who has reached perfection attains Brahma which is the highest state of knowledge. He can do so by controlling his mind with determination, giving up the objects of the senses, living in a secluded place and eating but little, overcoming passion, prejudice, egoism, violence, lust, anger, greed and arrogance. Reaching this state he neither grieves nor desires, is always cheerful, treats all beings alike and meditates on Me. He attains supreme devotion to Him and engaging in all kinds of actions is blessed with grace.

Abandon all man-made laws, Shri Krishna tells Arjuna, and surrender to Me.

Arjuna must fight because being a Kshatriya it is his duty to do so.

God demands of everybody to do his duty. He demands the same thing from Arjuna. He should trust in God, seek His shelter and he will thus attain the highest peace and His eternal abode.

Shri Krishna told Arjuna He had declared to him the most secret knowledge and now it was up to him to reflect and act upon it. Since he was very dear to Him, He would tell him what was good for him. Arjuna should have full faith in Him, be devoted to Him, show Him the fullest respect and thus be relieved from all his worries. The wisdom of the Gita, Shri Krishna said, is for the wise only. This knowledge could not be imparted to those who were not His devotees or who did not wish to learn.

He who explains the Gita to others will be saved. He who propagates the Gita will also be saved and so will be the one who studies and recites it. He who simply listens to the Gita with faith will also be freed from all sins and will reach the pious stage of superior existence.

Shri Krishna then asked Arjuna if he had heard his discourse with careful attention and if it had removed his confusion about right and wrong action, destroyed his ignorance and brought him enlightenment. Arjuna replied that indeed his confusion had been removed and his doubts cleared. He was now prepared to act according to Shri Krishna's instructions.

Sanjay, the charioteer of King Dhritarashtra who had been listening to the dialogue between Lord Krishna and Arjuna, said he was thrilled to hear from Shri Krishna Himself the highest mystery of Yoga. He rejoiced every time he remebered this marvellous discourse. He also remembered with great joy the wonderful form of the Lord. He was convinced that wherever there was

Krishna, the Lord of Yoga, and Arjuna, the arch bowman, there would be prosperity, victory, welfare and morality.

Om Tat Sat

Glossary

Atman	The self or the Supreme Soul, identical with God
Bhakti	Devotion, total dedication
Brahma	The Absolute, the eternal and the supreme Reality of Vedanta Philosophy.
Brahmins	The priestly class, one of the four castes of India, the others being Kshatriyas (warriors), Vaisyas (traders and agriculturists) and Sudras (manual workers).
Brighu	A great seer
Dakshana	Money and presents given to Brahmins with love and respect
Dharma	Literally that which holds together, the righteous path, that which determines conduct, righteousness and sense of right and wrong in a man.
Gunas	Qualities, the three inherent attributes of matter: Of pure rest (*Sattva*), activity and desire (*Rajas*) and inertia (*Tamas*).

Jivatma	Individual soul
Jnana	Wisdom or knowledge, spiritual realisation
Karma Yoga	The way of duty or work
Kshatriyas	Warriors, belonging to one of the four castes of India, the others being Brahmins, Vaisyas and Sudras.
Manu	The earliest law giver of India
Meru	A mythical mountain abounding in gold and other treasures
Moksha	Salvation, self-realisation
Narada	A divine seer
Nirvana	Annihilation of desire, passion and ego; liberation characterised by freedom and bliss.
Om	A mystic syllable, the most solemn of all words in India. It is usually placed at the beginning of sacred scriptures and is prefixed to prayers.
Om Tat Sat	Indicates the Supreme that is eternal or the Supreme Absolute Truth.
Purushottama	The most sacred word of the Vedas. It is the symbol of both of the personal God and the Absolute; an aid to concentration of thought.

Rajas	The quality of activity; one of the three *gunas* in the correlations of matter and nature.
Sannyasa	The vow of renouncing the world
Sattva	Wisdom; being in divine knowledge
Shastra	Any work of divine or accepted authority.
Shiva	God of destruction
Sudras	The lowest of the four castes in India, custodians of manual labour, the other three being the Brahmins (priestly class), the Kshatriyas (warriors), and Vaisyas (traders)
Tamas	Quality of inertia or dullness
Tyaga	Renunciation
Varuna	The lord of the ocean, usually associated with Mitra, and a form of the lord of the sun
Vaisyas	One of the four castes of India, the trading and agricultural community, the others being Brahmins, Kshatriyas and Sudras.
Vedas	The great scripture of the Hindus and the ultimate authority of the Hindu religion.

Vedanta	The philosophy of Vedanta affirms the existence of a single impersonal spiritual principle, the supreme conscious Brahma.
Vishwarupa	Wearing all forms, omnipresent, universal
Yama	God of death
Yoga	The way of union with God
Yogi	One who practises Yoga

Bibliography

1. The Song Celestial — *Sir Edwin Arnold (Shrimad Bhagavad Gita)*

2. Shri Bhagavad Gita-Rahasya. Vols. I & II — *B.G. Tilak*

3. Light from the Gita — *M.P. Pandit*
4. Gems from the Gita — *M.P. Pandit*
5. Gita the Mother — *Commentary by Dnyaneshwar Maharaj*

6. The Gita for Modern Man — *Krishna Chaitanya*

7. Bhagavd Gita — *Maharishi Mahesh Yogi*

8. Gita–The Mother — *M.K. Gandhi Edited by Jag Pravesh Chandra*

9. The Bhagavad Gita — *Geeta Press*
10. The Gospel of Selfless Action or The Gita According to Gandhi — *Mahadev Desai*
11. The Bhagavad Gita — *S. Radhakrishnan*
12. Bhagavadgita — *C. D. Deshmukh*
13. Bhagavad Gita — *Yogi Manohar*

157

Other Titles in the Series

ALL YOU WANTED TO KNOW ABOUT

Parapsychology/Spiritual Sciences

- Spiritualism in Day-to-Day Life
- The Prophecies of Nostradamus
- Spirituality
- Nostradamus
- Spiritual Healing
- Dowsing
- Psychic Development
- Aura
- Hypnosis

Personal Transformation

- Practical Approach to Reiki
- Tantra Yoga
- Karma Yoga
- Jnana Yoga
- Bhakti Yoga
- Hatha Yoga
- Relaxation
- Kriya Yoga
- Meditation
- Kundalini

- Chakras and Nadis
- Happiness
- Reiki
- Mantras

Self-Help & Success
- Body Language
- Gardening
- Etiquette
- Self Motivation
- Love and Relationships
- Secrets of Magic
- As a Man Thinketh
- Vedic Mathematics
- Stress & Anger
- Secret of Success
- Feng Shui
- I Ching
- Vastushastra
- Increasing Memory Power

For complete catalogue write to:
A-59 Okhla Industrial Area, Phase-II,
New Delhi-110020.
Tel: 26387070, 2 6386209
Fax: 91-11-26383788 E-mail: ghai@nde.vsnl.net.in